DEREK JETER

BASEBALL'S CAPTAIN

ABBE L. STARR

LERNER PUBLICATIONS ◆ MINNEAPOLIS

SPORTS THRILLS
MEET
RESEARCH SKILLS

Lerner SPORTS

Free Database Trial: **lernersports.com**

Lerner Publications Company
An imprint of Lerner Publishing Group, Inc.
241 First Avenue North
Minneapolis, MN 55401 USA

For reading levels and more information, look up this title at www.lernerbooks.com.

Main body text set in Myriad Pro Semibold. Typeface provided by Adobe.

Photo Editor: Annie Zheng

Library of Congress Cataloging-in-Publication Data

Names: Starr, Abbe L., author.
Title: Derek Jeter : baseball's captain / Abbe L. Starr.
Description: Minneapolis : Lerner Publications, [2023] | Series: Epic sports bios (Lerner sports) | Includes bibliographical references and index. | Audience: Ages: 7–11 | Audience: Grades: 4–6 | Summary: "Growing up, Derek Jeter dreamed of playing for the New York Yankees. His dream came true in 1995. Jeter starred for the Yankees for 20 seasons and helped the team win five World Series"— Provided by publisher.
Identifiers: LCCN 2022010081 (print) | LCCN 2022010082 (ebook) | ISBN 9781728476513 (library binding) | ISBN 9781728478555 (paperback) | ISBN 9781728482507 (ebook)
Subjects: LCSH: Jeter, Derek, 1974-—Juvenile literature. | Baseball players—United States—Biography—Juvenile literature.
Classification: LCC GV865.J48 S83 2023 (print) | LCC GV865.J48 (ebook) | DDC 96.357092 [B]—dc23/eng/20220408

LC record available at https://lccn.loc.gov/2022010081
LC ebook record available at https://lccn.loc.gov/2022010082

Manufactured in the United States of America
1-52232-50672-7/11/2022

TABLE OF CONTENTS

A STRONG START

On April 2, 1996, New York Yankees shortstop Derek Jeter stood at home plate. It was the first Major League Baseball (MLB) game of the season for the Yankees. They were down 1–0 against Cleveland.

Jeter gripped his bat in the fifth inning and waited for the pitch. He appeared calm as the ball whizzed toward him. *SMACK!* Jeter belted the ball over the left-field wall for a home run.

Jeter holds his bat high and keeps his eyes on the pitcher.

FACTS AT A GLANCE

Date of birth: June 26, 1974

Position: shortstop

League: MLB

Professional highlights: was drafted in the first round of the 1992 MLB draft; helped the Yankees win the World Series five times; became the Yankees all-time leader in hits

Personal highlights: grew up in Pequannock, New Jersey, and Kalamazoo, Michigan; was president of his high school's Latin Club; has three daughters with his wife, Hannah Davis Jeter

Later in the game, Jeter made a great catch. In the seventh inning, a short fly ball soared to center field. Everyone thought it would drop to the ground for a hit. Jeter sprinted and made an outstanding one-handed catch. "I never took my eyes off it," he said. "I had it all the way." New York won 7–1. What a way to start the season!

Jeter was only 21 years old. The team's fans were excited to see what their new shortstop could do. With Jeter leading the way, the Yankees had a bright future.

Jeter smacked 10 home runs during the 1996 MLB season.

YOUNG DREAMER

Derek Sanderson Jeter was born on June 26, 1974. His mother, Dorothy Jeter, was an accountant. His father, Charles Jeter, was a social worker. They taught Derek and his younger sister, Sharlee, to work hard for what they wanted.

Left to right: Dorothy, Derek, Sharlee, and Charles Jeter

Yankee Stadium in 1996. The team began playing in a brand-new stadium in 2009.

The Jeter family lived in Pequannock, New Jersey. They were less than an hour's drive from New York City's Yankee Stadium. When Derek was four, his family moved from New Jersey to Kalamazoo, Michigan.

Derek's family loved baseball. His grandmother was a big Yankees fan. She played catch with Derek and took him to his first baseball game.

Before Derek was born, his father played baseball at Fisk University in Nashville, Tennessee. He taught his son to play different positions on the field. He had been a shortstop at Fisk, so shortstop became Derek's favorite position.

Derek told his friends and family that he would play for the Yankees one day. Some of his friends didn't believe him. But that only made Derek work harder to prove them wrong.

Derek and his father have a close relationship.

HARD WORK

Derek's parents supported his dreams. They said he could do anything he wanted to do if he worked at it. And they told him not to make excuses if he failed.

Derek jogs in a Yankees uniform in 1992.

In high school, Derek listened to his parents' advice. As a freshman, he played shortstop on the varsity team. After Derek's sophomore year, he joined a summer traveling baseball team. At 15, he was the second-youngest player to ever make the team. Derek showed up early and stayed late on game days to get extra practice.

In 2011, Kalamazoo Central High School named its baseball field Derek Jeter Field.

WELCOME TO
DEREK JETER FIELD
HOME OF THE
Kalamazoo Central High School
MAROON GIANTS
Derek Jeter is a 1992 Kalamazoo Central Graduate

In 1992, Derek opened his senior baseball season with three home runs in his first seven at bats. In the field, his skills at shortstop continued to grow. When Derek threw the ball to first base, it flew more than 90 miles (145 km) per hour! In 23 games, Derek had 30 hits, four home runs, and 23 RBIs. He also stole 12 bases in 12 tries.

Derek broke many high school baseball records. The American Baseball Coaches Association and *USA Today* named him 1992 High School Player of the Year. Officials in Michigan named him the best high school player in the state. Derek's efforts brought him closer to his dream.

SCHOOL FIRST

Derek always wanted to be a baseball player. His parents told him to focus first on his schoolwork. If he didn't get good grades, he wouldn't be able to play. In high school, Derek was a member of the National Honor Society and became president of his school's Latin Club.

DREAM COME TRUE

On June 1, 1992, the Yankees chose Jeter in the first round of the MLB draft. He was 18, one of the youngest players on the Yankees rookie-level team. He was used to being younger than most of his teammates. But playing in the minor leagues was a big change from high school.

Jeter visits Yankee Stadium for the first time after being drafted by the team.

Jeter played for the Gulf Coast League Yankees. He had no hits in his first seven at bats, and he struck out five times. He had only struck out once during his entire senior year of high school.

Minor-league players were older and stronger than the players Jeter had faced in high school. The game moved faster. Jeter's coaches saw his skill and continued to support him. After the season, they moved him up a level to Class A.

Jeter throws the ball to first base during a 1993 spring training game. His throws usually hit their targets.

Jeter gets ready to catch the ball at second base.

Jeter worked hard with the Class A Greensboro Hornets. He soon found his stride. In an April 1993 game against the Augusta Pirates, the score was tied 9–9. Jeter swung and slammed a game-winning home run! His batting average and defense improved. In June, he played in the South Atlantic League All-Star Game.

Baseball America named Jeter the league's best defensive shortstop and its most exciting player. He won the Minor League Player of the Year award. In 1994, Jeter moved up two levels to the Class AAA Columbus Clippers.

On May 29, 1995, the Yankees needed an extra player. They chose Jeter! He played well in the field, but he struggled as a batter. The game was tied 7–7 in the 11th inning. A tiebreaking run waited on third base, and Jeter was up to bat. Yankees fans were excited, but Jeter struck out. He finished his season back in Columbus, Ohio, with the Clippers.

Jeter bats for the Columbus Clippers. Between 1992 and 1995, he played 447 games in the minor leagues.

MAJOR-LEAGUE WINNER

Jeter soon found success in the major leagues with the Yankees. In 1996, he was the team's starting shortstop. Jeter showed he was ready to be a star by blasting a home run in the first game of the season! New York beat Cleveland 7–1. Jeter later said, "My best opening day was my first one. . . . That will always be one of the most special games I've ever played."

Jeter warms up before a Yankees game.

The Yankees kept winning with Jeter at shortstop. Their success continued in the playoffs against the Texas Rangers and Baltimore Orioles. In the World Series, the Yankees faced the Atlanta Braves. In Game 6, Jeter scored a run and had an RBI in a 3–2 victory. The Yankees won the World Series! Jeter was the American League Rookie of the Year.

TURN 2 FOUNDATION

As a kid, Jeter had always looked up to pro athletes. After joining the Yankees, he wanted to do something positive with his fame. In 1996, he started the Turn 2 Foundation. The foundation promotes healthy lifestyles for children and helps them stay away from drugs and alcohol.

Jeter (*wearing number 2*) celebrates with teammates during the 1998 World Series. The Yankees beat the San Diego Padres in four games.

In 1998, the Yankees had the best record in MLB. They set an all-time team record with 114 wins. They were unstoppable with Jeter in the lineup. The Yankees won the World Series again! Jeter's 127 runs and 19 home runs set new season records for a Yankees shortstop.

Jeter continued to win big games and awards. He won his third World Series in 1999. In 2000, he became the first Yankees player to win the MVP award in the All-Star Game. The Yankees won their third championship in a row that year, and Jeter was the World Series MVP.

MR. NOVEMBER

On October 31, 2001, the Yankees played Game 4 of the World Series against the Arizona Diamondbacks. The score was tied 3–3 in the 10th inning. The game had stretched past midnight to become the first MLB game ever played in November. Jeter hit a game-winning home run and earned the nickname Mr. November.

YANKEES LEGEND

Fans loved Jeter's clutch hitting. They also enjoyed his great defense. On July 1, 2004, the Yankees played an extra-inning game against the Boston Red Sox. With two outs and a runner at third, Boston hit the ball to the left side of the field.

Jeter gets a hit during the 2000 MLB All-Star Game. He won the All-Star Game's MVP award.

Jeter sprinted to the ball and made a running catch near the seats. He couldn't stop and flew into the first few rows. Jeter cut his chin and needed stitches, but the Red Sox didn't score. New York finally won the game in the 13th inning.

Jeter flies into the seats after making a catch against the Red Sox.

Shortstop is one of the most demanding positions on a baseball field. Jeter worked hard to master the position.

In 2003, the Yankees made Jeter their team captain thanks to his leadership and great play. Beginning in 2004, he won five Gold Glove Awards as the best fielding shortstop in the American League. He also became the Yankees all-time hits leader and broke the record for most career hits for a shortstop. In November 2009, Jeter won his fifth World Series.

On July 9, 2011, Jeter became the 28th MLB player to reach 3,000 career hits. During the next few seasons, he

had several injuries. In 2013, he played in only 17 games. Getting back in shape from his injuries was the most difficult part of his career. Jeter said, "There are no short-cuts when it comes to training; you have to do the work if you want to see the results." He decided that 2014 would be his last MLB season.

Jeter makes a catch for an out.

Jeter smiles at a display honoring his uniform number on Derek Jeter Day.

The mayor of New York City declared September 7, 2014, to be Derek Jeter Day. Fans at Yankee Stadium celebrated Jeter's life and career. He played his last game in New York on September 25. The game was tied in the ninth inning. Jeter gave his fans one last thrill with a game-winning hit.

In July 2016, Jeter married Hannah Davis. They have three daughters, Bella Raine, Story Grey, and River Rose. But Jeter wasn't finished with MLB. From 2017 to 2022, he was a co-owner of the Miami Marlins.

On September 8, 2021, Jeter joined the National Baseball Hall of Fame. He spoke to his daughters during his speech. He told them they could achieve their dreams if they worked hard enough.

Jeter and his wife at a ceremony in 2017 to retire his uniform number. To honor Jeter, no Yankees player will wear number 2 again.

Jeter always dreamed of playing for his favorite team. "There was only one thing I wanted to be," he said. "Shortstop for the New York Yankees." Through his entire baseball career, Jeter worked hard and played with passion. He achieved his dream and so much more.

Career hits: 3,465

Career home runs: 260

Career RBIs: 1,311

World Series champion: 1996, 1998, 1999, 2000, 2009

Gold Glove Awards: 2004, 2005, 2006, 2009, 2010

GLOSSARY

at bat: a turn at batting

batting average: a figure found by dividing the number of official times at bat into the number of base hits

captain: a player who is the official leader of a team

clutch: successful in important moments and games

draft: when teams take turns choosing new players

extra inning: an inning played when a baseball game is tied after nine innings

minor league: a pro baseball league that is not a major league

MVP: short for Most Valuable Player

RBI: short for run batted in, a run in baseball that is driven in by a batter

rookie: a first-year player

shortstop: a baseball player usually positioned between second and third base

varsity: the top team at a school

SOURCE NOTES

6   Connor Kiesel, "Looking Back: Jeter's Milestone Opening Day in
    Cleveland," Fox Sports, July 9, 2014, https://www.foxsports.com
    /ohio/story/new-york-yankees-derek-jeter-first-home-run
    -cleveland-indians-opening-day-1996-070914.

17   Derek Jeter, *Derek Jeter: Jeter Unfiltered* (New York: Gallery Books,
    2014), 54.

24   Jeter, 74.

27   Matthew Roberson, "Derek Jeter Inducted into Hall of Fame:
    'It's Been a Hell of a Ride,'" *New York Daily News*, September 8,
    2021, https://www.nydailynews.com/sports/baseball
    /yankees/ny-derek-jeter-hall-of-fame-speech-20210908
    -4zv4ifq4pbe55b5l63z776653y-story.html.

LEARN MORE

Derek Jeter's Turn 2 Foundation
https://www.mlb.com/turn-2-foundation

Fishman, Jon M. *Inside the New York Yankees*. Minneapolis: Lerner Publications, 2022.

Karpovich, Todd. *Derek Jeter and the New York Yankees*. Minneapolis: Sports Zone, 2019.

Lowe, Alexander. *G.O.A.T. Baseball Shortstops*. Minneapolis: Lerner Publications, 2022.

MLB Kids
https://www.mlb.com/fans/kids

Sports Illustrated Kids—Baseball
https://www.sikids.com/baseball

INDEX

PHOTO ACKNOWLEDGMENTS

Image credits: Focus On Sport/Getty Images, pp. 4, 17; Andrey_Popov/Shutterstock, pp. 5, 28; Rich Pilling/MLB/Getty Images, p. 6; Jim McIsaac/Getty Images, p. 7; AP Photo/ Marty Lederhandler, p. 8; John Roca/NY Daily News/Getty Images, p. 9; Diamond Images/ Getty Images, pp. 10, 14, 15, 24; AP Photo/Joel Bissell/Kalamazoo Gazette, p. 11; Steve Crandall/Getty Images, p. 13; AP Photo/Ken Babbitt/Four Seam Images, p. 16; Doug Pensinger/Allsport/Getty Images, p. 19; AP Photo/Ed Reinke, p. 21; AP Photo/Frank Franklin II, p. 22; Steve Grayson/WireImage/Getty Images, p. 23; Elsa/Getty Images, p. 25; Rich Schultz/Getty Images, p. 26; AP Photo/Hans Pennink, p. 27.

Design elements: saicle/iStock/Getty Images.

Cover: AP Photo/Paul Sancya (top); AP Photo/Kathy Willens (bottom).